The Bride Minaret

Akron Series in Poetry

Akron Series in Poetry
Mary Biddinger, Editor

The Bride Minaret

Heather Derr-Smith

*Heathen
(Heather Derr-
Smith)*

 Čuvajse. org

The University Of Akron Press
Akron, Ohio

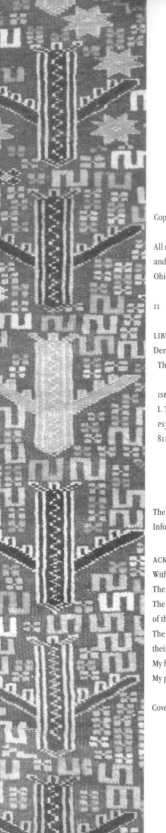

All rights reserved ❧ First Edition 2008 ❧ Manufactured in the United States of America. ❧ All inquiries and permission requests should be addressed to the Publisher, The University of Akron Press, Akron, Ohio 44325-1703.

11 10 09 08 07 5 4 3 2 1

LIBRARY OF CONGRESS CATALOGING-IN-PUBLICATION DATA
Derr-Smith, Heather.
  The bride minaret / by Heather Derr-Smith. — 1st ed.
    p. cm. — (Akron series in poetry)
  ISBN 978-1-931968-57-7 (pbk. : alk. paper)
  I. Title.
  PS3604.E7546B75 2008
  811'.6—DC22

                          2008025959

The paper used in this publication meets the minimum requirements of American National Standard for Information Sciences—Permanence of Paper for Printed Library Materials, ANSI z39.48–1984. ∞

ACKNOWLEDGMENTS
With thanks to the following:
The editors at *Margie,* where "Evening, Mount Vernon, Iowa" first appeared.
The Vermont Studio Center for their generous fellowship, which provided the space and time for many of these poems to be written.
The Mount Vernon Writers' Group, especially Barbara Lau, Marianne Taylor, and Emory Gillespie, for their encouragement and support.
My family, especially my parents, who loved me deeply and truly.
My partner, Todd Smith, who stuck with it.

Cover: Image courtesy of warrug.com.

Contents

3. Histories

To Owen, the one Jesus loved best

Strangers (Ghuraba)

In the front pocket of his jeans were beads:

> garnet, carnelian, amber, turquoise.

He meant to give them to a friend, bed made

In a Berlin hospital, the hand he held,

> so lightweight—

A white plastic thimble

> on his friend's forefinger,

To catch and thread

> the frail beats of his heart.

A red bead of light glowed at the end, listening with its red ear

For life, going out.

> No one knew he was sick

Until a month before he died.

The beads were Bedouin, a gift from his mother,

Before, when she named him her son.

Shadows line the narrow Damascene streets.

> Roasted chestnuts,

The milky juice made from orchids,

Remind him of his friend, now dead.

                              The beads

Returned to the front pocket of his jeans,
                                        flecks of light
From two loves, one a mother turned away,

one just gone.

The Lord hath said, I can withdraw the shadows anytime I wish.

He meant it as a threat.

The beads of light strike like matches

Of memory,
                from desert to Berlin to here, and the light

Is so full of questions.

In the Great Umayyad Mosque,
                                they framed the questions and the light
In niches,
                the place of appearing, a lamp

Dangling above in unceasing desire
                                like the yearning of graffiti

Left by strangers on the walls of old Damascene houses:

                                The doves of the thick forest cry for me
The lightning strikes
                        The rain falls on the horizon
                                                —unreachable.

He remembered the long walk with his mother to the mosque

When he was too young to go so far, crossing the choked traffic,

Navigating through.

How do you keep going? he asked his mother.

She said, The Bedouin keep going until the sweat runs like pearls.

Now a man, he follows the path,
                              but it goes forward and then back,

And he is back in the hospital room,
                              surrounded by the lighted lamps of memory,

Back further to the night of a party, sheets starched with semen.

2.

Go,

Get a gift from every person in the village:
                              thyme, raisins, fig, a bag of soil.

From Berlin, a tab of ecstasy, a cocktail umbrella, a postcard of Vermeer,

A woman bathed in light.
                    It's dangerous, this direction.
Dawish the Palestinian said,

                    My homeland is not a traveling bag. But mine is.
When the Bedouins would hear
                    the creaking of waterwheels in the garden of a house,

It reminded them of the mournful groans of camels.

Or was it the other way around?

Which way is home?

I am like a person with many souls, each clinging to a different place.

(I can no longer talk of myself as if I were not present.)

I was the one who held his hand.

It was my hands on his back, a month before—

The party had not yet ended.

I saw him pass through the hall.

So many friends have we, wanderers!

But our house is inhabited with *al-Wahdah,*

which means lonely.

The lamps are lit along the streets of Damascus,

the smell of diesel

But the memory of the smell of elderberry.

The alleys lead to secret spaces,

porticos, arcades,

The architecture of worship

where *martyrs of love* go and hide.

We want

Latticed windows like the ones in Basra

decorated with glass.

I get down on my knees

                    in the direction of the Ka'ba,

Where ex nihilo the world emanates,

                    an embryo, motherless.

Every time I get down on my knees

                    in front of a stranger,

I am congealed with fear,

                    like John Chrysostom when he was young,

Who found the book of magic

                    floating down the river

And, though it was forbidden,

                    opened and read.

The Jesus minaret and the Bride minaret

                    rocket into the sky congested with soot.

The towers are lit

              and point the way ahead: *to be merciful, to forbid*

To receive   *to reverse*   Which is it?

The only way to know is to close the book and not look back.

At the end of the world, the women will be clothed naked.

I've seen her already,

                                          fugitive bride.

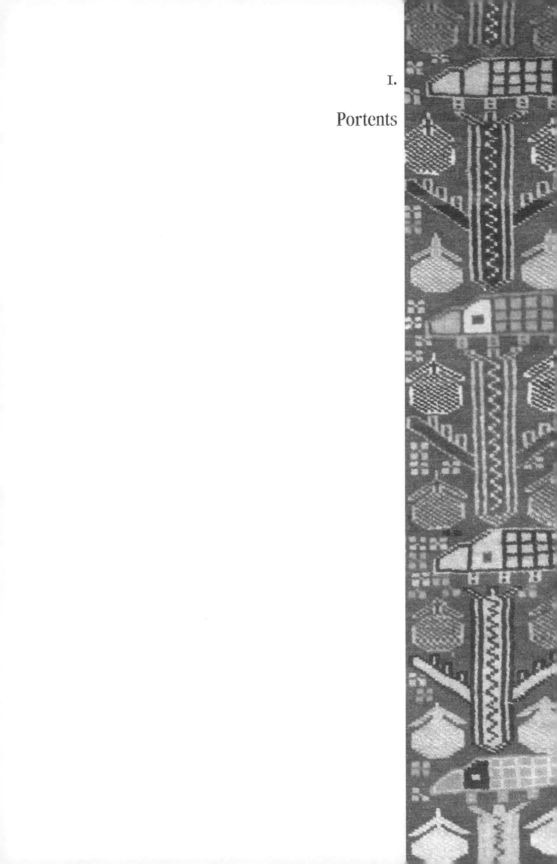

I.

Portents

Cover

Osage trees line the gravel road going nowhere.
We gather hedge apples because they ward off spiders.

The wood is tougher than most, makes good fences.

The ducks, meanwhile, are copulating wildly in the pond.
Frog sperm floats on the surface of the water. The fancy man
Dunks the plain lady in filth, drowning her like the witches in Canterbury,

The ones who wouldn't confess, and the ones who did.

This is the house on the farm where we first lived, when the tornado
Came and picked me up out of the car, knocking out my wind in the ditch,

Sucking on the back of a Mennonite girl's neck as I hunched to cover her.

The wind kept me from running in my dreams. The windows of a stranger's house
Blew in. The glass jingled on the floor like party drinks.

We kicked the door in together out of shock.

Back home, the roof was gone, but in the basement the baby slept in his swing
To the tick-tick of unstoppable small motors.

I never did see that Mennonite girl again. Untrue!
I saw her every week at the Piggly Wiggly, and she never did acknowledge me.

One Season from Another

A puzzle of broken ice, the clouds and their modesty,
The corpse like winter trees and their secrets, this is
One season.
              There is somebody who cuts up bodies with a saw
Like lumber and kindling. This person is called an articulator.

In Vermont, there were always high walls of firewood,
Just in case, and widows did all the work with the fire.

Newspaper story: a conflagration of a pregnant woman,
The blackened curl of unborn child, a question of decency,

The clouds again. The covering of sky is so claustrophobic,
Struggling to break free from the ground. My body is stepping

Out of shadows. The newspaper turns its pages into late May.
The widows still swing their axes in the yard with its sudden

Gaiety of little yellow flowers. Rain floods the pasture.
Owen throws his whole body down into dirty water.

What kind of mother am I? Don't find me out.
I'll cover myself with ten thousand sequins.

The sun argues with my boy: undress. He agrees. His body
Like a scrap of blanched sky, fallen in the water, collop of my flesh

Giggling in the flood.

Boundary Waters

My guide to this place points out the pitcher plants,
Red as the top of a Coca-Cola bottle,
Doubled over laughing as I pass.

The birches peel their skins off as I do my scabs.
Each one keeps trying to get out of life but can't.
They are afraid of heights.

The bog has hold of my legs and won't let go.
It's jealous. There is a river under there that flows backwards.
There is no way I can get out.

My cell phone rings impossibly at this moment, signalless.
This is taken as a sign.
My three-year-old son cries for me and is gone.

The tamarack trees blaze yellow in warning.
My guide has gone away in more than one direction.
There is a gate-closing panic in the eagles' wingbeat above me.

Thunder Snow, Montpelier, Vermont

The lightning is another plate shattering.
They are horn mad at each other in myth's kitchen.

My armpits smell like tamales.
It's so cold outside that ice needles float in the air.

Down the hill in the valley, a man writes a letter
And says goodbye to everyone he loves.

We will find him in the morning on channel 9. Tonight
Nobody has the news. But look, someone has footage

Of a leg blown off in an explosion, Baghdad: fronds of flesh
Like a fern, unfurling. It's not shown on the television.

Owen cries in a fever. I lift him up in my arms
And spray his hot body with milk from my breasts.
The thunder gets quiet just like in the theater.

Now the snow is left alone to fill the world softly.
It is finished, said the hanging man,
And there's not an ear to hear it.

Evening, Mount Vernon, Iowa

Marvels at the darkness of a storm.

Walking over the fields toward the edge of the world.

Chimney swifts beat their alternate wings, or bats.

Owen rescues worms from drowning in puddles.

This is a small town in Iowa, like the kind in *Sleeping with the Enemy.*

A girl about six stands in the middle of the street, twirling a ball on a string.

Its tail flashes in silver-pink and purple glitter. It hisses: faster, faster.

The sound scares Owen, who rushes down the sidewalk, catching his toe on a crack.

He wails.

The sun, a lump of light, falls behind the baseball bleachers.

The wisteria smells like honey.

I shake out the water from the plastic pool to ward off West Nile.

Rockville Pike

Civic's caught in the river of traffic running down the District,
Chevy Chase, Bethesda, into the pinball lights
Of neon strip malls and God-lit car dealerships.
Reflections smear up the hood and over the man's face.

A line of people snake away from the velvet rope
Of Chez Palestine, its script-lettered sign, like Arabic.

Two angelic-muscled bouncers at the gate.

Are you ready to order? The waiter waits.
The candlelight flickers. The sous-chef chops anonymously.

In the parking lot, teenagers weave in and out of cars.
A boy tightrope-walks a curb.
There is the scrape and clack of a skateboard.

The Civic remembers its childhood.
There is no turning back. Valet,
Go and get it.

Star Chamber

There is hyssop in the dark in the ditch.
I walked down there to get flowers with my husband.
Our shoes smelled ancient and medicinal for a long time after.

There are farm machines that look like spacecraft with spotlights
And drown out the stars above. You know what they are called,
The machines with names like pets and attachments.
You look like a Hutterite boy in a cowboy hat
And paisley shirt with silver snaps. Irresistible.

When we get to the lake, you push me under the water.
The waves wash me up in an imaginary bikini.
I put my fingers in your mouth, and you push me under.

The sky is biled with clouds.
We are driving home through the northern fields.
I have dreams of winnowing forks.

I am locked up in the morning with a bolt over my heart.
They'll take my baby and throw him against a passing train.
This is a short story that ends in stoning.

Blessing

Drinking "Frutti" and "Thumbs Up!" in the courtyard of Kali Temple, Calcutta.
The priest told us to tie an ochre-red stone to a tree. We did, young
Husband and wife, and knelt in prayer for a child-of-our-own.

In the University of Iowa Hospital, Pitocin dripped from a bag.
We were made to. Pushing a body out of my flesh and into fluorescence.
My anus bloomed like a pink carnation.

One doctor, a beautiful woman, cheered. The other one was angry.
I was a stethoscope of apology, so sorry, so sorry. I arched up

To put my lips around his ear: *It's all my fault*. But what I meant to say
Was pure hatred, the kind that locked up Eden with its lab-coated angel-guards.

I don't catch my babies, said the man, his necklace of little heads swinging.
I squat, shitting in his empty pocket, and lift my baby onto my blood-red breast.

Gift

The rain smells of almonds and the surprise
Of green snakes in the garden.

Owen sits in his high chair with a Babar
Café au lait bowl full of Malt-O-Meal, eats it all,

Pushing the bowl over the edge. Done.
It breaks into two pieces of jagged porcelain.

It was a gift I bought in Paris
After the Charlie Chaplin festival

And the stranger I kissed by an unnamed canal.
The stranger, too, was unnamed, and we didn't speak.

I didn't know then, nor do I understand now
Why I followed him and why I opened my mouth,
Except
                for the pleasure of it.

Ten years before Owen was born.

I give him gifts he knows nothing of,
Will never be remembered.

Have I missed any shards hidden
In the carpet? Will they cut his fat feet later?

I hold the bowl, each half in a hand, an open belly.
To him it is only two chunks of whiteness, a nursery rhyme.

Happy he broke it, he says, *I did it.*

Tiffany Blues

Owen nurses his plastic baby
At his naked chest, the cock of his head,
The question mark at the end of lovemaking.

I love the two scars that are his nipples,
Their impossibility.

He drops the baby and climbs the piano bench,
Opens my purse, lining the credit cards
In perfect plastic rows,

And a small Tiffany's box in robin's egg blue:
Tiny diamond earrings fall to the floor.

He watches them almost drift,
Little pricks of light like salt through the air.
I want to discern their meaning: give me
Some alomancy before they hit
With two needles' specks of sound: that's it.

He wants everything from me: the box is his,
The blue, the smallest flicker of a crystal.
This is our one single world without edges.

He believes that we are together in the never-ending
Of a fairytale.

I pick up the diamonds. He wants the Tiffany box.
But I take it and put it up on the shelf.
It's mine. He cannot reach it.

Bloom

Owen smells of gardenias tonight,
Preteen vacations in Hawaii
With my mother the Braniff girl,
Swirled breast to thigh in Pucci,
Her orange go-go boots and clear,
Plastic astronaut-inspired bubble
Encasing her red hair in case
Of inclement weather. Womanhood

Begins with Estée Lauder Christmas
Gift sets and gardenia perfume:
                    Amarige de Givenchy.

Owen is curled under my arm
Like a nautilus, the corners
Of his mouth turned down in a deep
Frown of sleep.
His ear, open to my breath, cups
The fluid dark of the room into it.
His eyes glow like coins; his nightgown
Is a swatch of moonlight. In his bed
In Iowa, we are far, far from the sea,
Infibulated against water's penetration.
My little boy, a dark shadow
Of that tropical flower, now blooming,
A piece of woman, of mother, and me.

Trans/Substance

She preaches in the expat church, Sunday morning after a dinner party
In which a prominent lawyer had made advances. He was impressed

With her bravery. From the pulpit, her voice is full of something on the verge
Of panic, which is exactly what she knows about God. Ten years after the siege

When bodies were snapped like Pop Rocks in God's mouth, Sarajevo
Is *the* place to be: porn stars, poets, queers, Islamists, and Christian musicians.

She's a woman of the cloth, a life for Him, *My Life to Live*. She's always wanted
To be a prostitute, dance around a pool table in black and white.

Godard sits down in the congregation. The whole discussion gets ridiculous.
She is not a Frenchwoman. She's never been gifted at glossolalia.

She does not understand the two sides of everything. She actually finds the hijab
Attractive, the way it frames the face. She knows frames are dangerous.

She dreams of walking like a grim reaper through the Bascarsija, her heels
Clicking the cobblestones, perfectly beautiful under her burka.

Ten years ago, she was reading Hemingway and dreamt of being a partisan
Who only spoke in very short sentences.

Now she visits the Amsterdam Prostitution Welcome Center web site
for more Information. We're not in Iowa anymore.

She blesses the congregation. They file out and say, *Good job*. The refugees pay her
In cigarettes they force her to smoke. They'll kill her. Here's the body, here's the blood,

Bite me.

Blow

A soldier in a *Free Winona* T-shirt glares at me from under the sign to Pale,
Leaving Sarajevo. We cannot know each other. He'll tell me an old story
I've heard already, appeal to saints (Arkan and George) and blowjobs.
I'm not listening. It's the same old turbofolk they sing at Galeria Ko
Behind the curtain of smoke. Turn off the televisions in the shops,
Their daylight porn standards. Close the book of magic. All the magazines
They sell now are obscene. I just want to call my friend on her cell phone,
But nothing works in the Balkans, they say. This is a lie.
Look at the blue ballroom of sky and swinging cloud skirts too high above
The mountains to snag. There is no fog today. The phone works fine. It's not working.
The Balkan metaphor is a cliché that slurs like a paramilitary tiger on slijvovici.
Replay: the tired old songs of men wearing berets in a pit (on vinyl!) or in the bandstand,
And the soldier boy under the sign to Pale.

A widow tells me I am too cold.
She points this out to me. She has the same missing teeth
Depicted in a satirical travel book. She has never read this book. Neither
Has her son who wears a wool sweater. As for me, they say
My son is not right. His vampire teeth sink into the neck of me.
He has never been to Bosnia or Transylvania. He lies in a bed at home,
Far from massacres and temptations. There are signs of mercury
Poisoning: Bronchiectasis, walking on tiptoes, rage. This is not an emergency.
It's been a long time coming. My son would love war.
How many eyes watch from the yards when he dances, throwing his body
Like *Man in Instant Death*.
I pray to a weeping virgin on the Catholic side of Bosnia. I'll say,
Thank you for all the wars that have made life so meaningful.
I feel as if I've come home. Genocide always has that effect on me.

I will pass this story down to my son, a souvenir,
Like those pretty copper shell casings inscribed in the Bascarsija. If you lick it,
It tastes exactly like blood. Everyone knows this is true. And if you say it's true,
It *is* true. That's what prayer is and poetry. The poets make the best war criminals.
The truth is, poets are liars.
And prayer? Get down on your knees and suck.

Bit

Chartreuse-colored bruises spot my body.
There are quarter-sized imprints, rings of desire.

Accident: Owen's small foot in the tub slips,
Kicking into my vagina, small rip.

Deliberate: He wants to eat me. I say: No biting.
But he does.

One day this one I love could kill me, if he wanted.
He weighs now thirty pounds, yet the force he is

Can push me underwater in the bath, can frighten me
Already at the possibilities.

Beloved

He picks her up in his car, midday,
The sun fatiguing all the blue
From the air, hushed up against the dust.

They take the back road with *The Passion
Of St. John* on the radio. He's the one
Jesus loved best.

They go fast over the hillocks,
Past rows of corn, God in the rows:
This one, that one, this one, that one,

Stop and get out in the place where a cougar was.

He pulls her down, lays her over the arc
Of the earth in an alley of mowed grass,
Queen Anne's lace and morning glories
Like pieces of lingerie caught on the barbed wire
Fence. Wolf spiders jump back into husks
Of corn, opening and folding like prayers
Whispered over golden teeth.

They found a bear nearby in early spring,
Impossible to imagine.
When they sliced his belly open, it was full
Of water insects, a terrible smell.

She goes down
Under him, sees monarch butterflies frantic for places she'll never go,
And small insignificant flowers about to die
Poke out their heads,
                    the color of Christ's robes.

Chador

The little boy's toes are folded upon each other like lovers,
Ten lovers, each pair in a huddle in a row.

They are ducking from planes that fly low.
He is singing a love song like his mother sang:

I am a flower in Botan, Garden of Eden.
I am a luminous jewel in Kurdistan's night.

As she covered her son with her body, like a robe, it
Slipped off.

The song was in a language of poetry
That froze into flesh and stiffened:

                              A fire with no ash is my heart that is in flame.
A fire with no ash is my heart that is burning.

The boy is a child running around a country on the television.
Fire covers the woman in the center of the world
From head to toe

Like an expensive coat,
Peeling the skin, revealing what law

Does not allow, down to the center O—
Black chador, eyeless even.

Throat and Lungs

1. Tonsils

Owen wipes the drool from his chin.
His chest is wet-rashed. It's hard to swallow.

He runs along the path kicking at puffballs,
Fungi exhaling dusts. Tomorrow he will

Cry, God-punched,
Waking in the foxfire light of recovery.

I will try to comfort him, holding his trembling
Body, as he struggles out of the anesthesia sleep.

I saw him go down under a costume of death
After they placed the mask over his mouth.

They cut out his tonsils and adenoids,
A bright pink pair of lymphoidal tissue laid on

A blue surgical sheet. The surgeon,
A dark-humored woman,
Drew around the lumps of flesh
The black outline of balloons
Held by a smiling clown.

2. Pertussis

When Owen came into the world, he slept
Uncontrollably. The nurse lifted him under

His armpits into the air and said to me, *See,
Something is wrong with this baby.* She shook him

Side to side, and he swayed like a long-legged doll
But would not awaken.

They pricked his heel and shot him in pale thighs.
Soundlessly, he slept on. His eyes were sewn shut

With tiny threads. His lips were a pink Arabic script,
Unopened. A cough leapt up his throat one night,

The size of a door slam. It picked him up like an angry father
Throwing him against the bed. He coughed out his soul:
Hijacked, or stolen.

The ambulance came with its sirens of life and urgency:
Hurry, hurry. The whole world did what they said,

Spiraled down around his limp body, breathless, still
Anchor. He slipped back into his skin

Seamlessly, eyes opened, a gift from death,

Given, returned, regiven.

Wake

Under the weight of twenty-four quarts
Of applesauce, the card table bows.

The tractor growls down the drive.

Danger fans out behind
The mother, like the train of a wedding dress.

Tiny bird's head
Sits decapitated in a Dixie Cup.

The boys' boots are mud-caked on the steps.
Eyes flit like frightened

Bird wings. Their brother is dead,
Baby boy. Don't think

They haven't seen this before.
The neighbors drive up:

The gravel kicked in cold dust of ghosts.
The baby in a white gown

Is put in the bathroom on a table,
His jaw: horribly slack.

The lookers say he's beautiful.
The boys stand beside his cold body.

They saw his nipples, before they dressed him.
They won't answer to the sound of names.

Where has Owen gone? He is on the swing
Outgrowing him already.

And a deep hole descends in the ground.
He is too young to be alone in the yard.

He was too young to be alone in the yard.
We must not think they are the only ones.

Picnic with Laptop, British Columbia

She uses different colors of yarn to catch the salmon.

They fight like children, unsharing, mutilating one another.

Owen is watching Thomas trash-talk Percy on YouTube.

The Sleeping Beauty Mountains are sprawled against the blue robe of sky.

The mother dreams of putting it all into his mouth: roasted chestnuts,

Nanaimo Bars, fresh dragon eyes plucked from the stem.

She dreams he's growing into the feast, the five thousand, the boy with the fish.

He doesn't want it. He wants to watch it again, but the battery dies.

Mommy catches the salmon, big as a child, with frantic, bulging eyes.

Owen is frightened. He wants her breasts.

Put the fish away, Mommy, only be with me.

The table is laid: Cotechino with pistachios, gypsy salami, salmon.

He will eat none of it, and neither will we.

Mother's Day

What day is it when cotton from the cottonwood

Floats through the air

It must be long past spring

The rain's applause

The mothers at the playground are grieving or angry

I think they are angry with *me*

When I make conversation, they tell me about the morning news

The inscrutable question of motherhood: How could she drown all five of them

What did she see

The filigree of autumn leaves

                         veins that collapse into color

It wasn't me after all

                  I am relieved

We are all relieved that there had been signs and symptoms

Evening news

Luxuriant stars on an Iowa night

None excuses   not one

Each tick of light   each flash of beauty
                      pitiless

The Bell

The women who meet at the elementary school have big dogs.
Their whole houses look like Pottery Barn, smell like dog breath.
They must have some tenderness to have such large animals.
But I've seen their cages.

The children spill out of the school in every direction,
Searching for mothers. The dogs leap up and knock the children down.
The children pull on the women's legs: *Home, go home.*
But the women's smiles are like slivers of bone floating in space,
Immovable.

At the crosswalk is one—
Her hair is a radiant red lamp. There's an invisible brush, ever poised.
She reflects the sun through the Volvo windows,
The bones of her teeth bite the air when she laughs. At home,
The phone is laughing back like a bitch off the hook.

When my mother dies, I'll change into a man
Living in women's clothes. I have a collection of Nanette Lepore dresses.
I'll go breastless.
She always said there is such a wide gulf separating this world from that.
She won't see me. I'll run like a man running like a woman.

The dogs whimper and pule through browned teeth.
Their claws click on the sidewalk, chasing after killdeers flapping
Out their faked injuries.
The children circle like rocks broken off a planet, abandoned
To orbit forever. They can never return.

She must be entirely made of pearl-colored bone. And it isn't just her.
There are multiples, an entire gynarchy of the playground.
The bell rings, the dogs growl. There is a garden, somewhere, with almond trees.
I am not allowed to enter in.

2.

Prophecies

Traffic, Downtown Damascus

In the Manara Disco, the girls have gone.

The pole stands alone in the strobe—

Afterimage on the retina—

Saudi men in for the weekend,
                              the girls danced awkwardly on a stage too big for them.

Martyr's Square, Al-Merjeh,
                    Would you like a cup of tea?

Nut and juice shops frame the sidewalks.

                              Sidestreets lead to *farfoud*, very young girls.
The shoeshine boys call and call.
                              They will be at it all night.
Mini-cabs rove through the dark,
                              interiors lit with gaudy sequins and strewn

With plastic flowers, a porcelain Dutch figurine and windmill on the dashboard—

Drivers cry out for rides to the suburbs, Jeramana, with its Pentecostal churches

                              sputtering prayers the Muslims call tongues of djinns.

            A cheap teddy bear on the bed, the kind you buy at dollar shops—

Berze, with balconies of Kurdish insurgents
                              leaning into the heat of the night, glow

Of cigarette butts,

        newborn babies screaming their poetry of protests,

                a kimono painted with marsh and crane—

On to Sayeda Zainab where they cry for Husein, night after night,

The same old song, like the song of breath or blood beating.

Buds of breasts—the girls are everywhere.

Iraqi-Style Fish Shop, Damascus

The fish are opened up like salad bowls,
Slid between the metal bars of baskets,
Roasted in the wood-fired ovens, Iraqi style.
The flesh glows as if it were made of glass.
The men gather. Their fingers pull pieces of bread
From one giant flat loaf, as round as a bass drum.

His wife collapsed when she saw his skin,
Purple and green like a tie-dyed shirt.
His daughter erupts in tears, and she is only four.
A bird hops in its cage and sings to the streets below.
The oldest girl says, *See, I have found this in the refuse*,
A bicycle pump to inflate her ball.
See, these are the shoes I brought from Iraq,
silver football shoes. She wears them only in secret.

Naranj is a small bitter orange used to heal.
It grows in the courtyard, resisting the concrete.
We call the orange a *Portugal*
Because the sweet orange came from Portugal.
This is interpretation in the House of War.

The Ummah Is Changing is written on my chocolate bar.
The flavor is Ummah Orange.
These are the delights of the House of War.
Back home, the dense orange groves were scorched.
Through the warren of alleyways
And cinderblock homes was an incense of burnt oranges,
Burnt blossoms, burnt Portugal.

You can still buy those little Ramadan happy meals we used to love.
Mubarek Olsen, with little zombie children praying.
Remember the birds everyone kept in cages?
No one keeps birds like that in Europe anymore. It isn't humane.

The Girl Named *Tents,* Tanf Refugee Camp

1.

The girl dreams of a palliation of night over black Bedouin tents,

houses of goat hair—

The girl dreams of palaces from her UNHCR tent,

Canvas flaps whipping in the wind.

The tents—

Hundreds of them beat like cream-colored hearts, bloodless.

The girl was born into her people's journey.

It was hard to learn her own name

Because she belonged to so many.

The women named her *Khiyam,* which means *Tents,* because that is the state

She was born into.

She was supposed to be a boy, as all girls are.

At night, she listens to the whispered epithets of scorpions scratching in the sand.

The wind lifts its hackles and howls.

2.

The morning wind chafes against the tents with promises. By afternoon, it is humiliated.

When she picks up a rock from the edge of the road, she sees a suspicion of color,

A faint rose.

        She dreams of rosewater.

It is hard to breathe when the wind

Grips her young body. She is nine years old and beginning to know.

But dreams continue to cudgel her, bit by bit, stone by stone,

Knocking her off balance.

             The wind writes its calligraphy in invisible ink.

The grains of sand strike together in tiny melodies.

            Only the dogs can hear the highest pitch.

The boys chase the dogs, hurling stones.

The girls wince against the blowing dirt.

The edges of their eyes are like the shores of the Mediterranean.

Their lashes are waves that never stop reaching.

She has never seen the Mediterranean, but she dreams of its blue light.

3.

Khiyam dreams of God.

        She names him *You.*

Back in the tent is a rare quiet, like the spaces between writing. She's afraid to step there.

Desire links and unlinks back to *You.*

Desire is passed from lip to lip like the Huffaz,

the ones who memorized and recited *You* before you were written.

4.

To write my love, I need a reed from Iraq,

a knife with an edge like a razor.

At night, after the dust clouds settle down to the ground
and the fires die,
The sky is soot, lamp-black ink
strained through silk.

Alif by *alif,*

Every bone in the camp is bound together like the stitching on a codex.

I live in my tent surrounded by forms of you:

Djinns that shape-shift in your images.

Every tent has a name, and every name is the breath of you.

At night the wind ties its knots and loosens them,

Constricts the throat, then releases its sighing.

I seek refuge with the Lord of Dawn.

                                        The stars are silver rosettes entwined on a black bush.

As the dawn lifts, the light weaves red and pink, the colors of the madder root.

Everyone wants to write to you.

They are pulling up all the reeds in Iraq.

No one can stop all the ink from flowing.

Internally Displaced

On the streets of Cairo beside a mountain of trash, the diesel fumes
And dirty children smell like her version of events, unaltered.

She collects labels of Prada handbags when they're all identical.

In the mega-cities, constant waves of people and dogs coming and going over garbage,
It's a fashion set. The street children are supermodels. They make the world shudder.

She drinks Roo-Ahfzah Punch every Ramadan, mulberry juice in Bab Touma—
Back home, she's spins with all the options in the Safeway aisle, spends her weekends
In Boystown, Chicago, cinnamon rolls at Ann Sather's after ecstasy—
Bollywood on Devon Avenue, beggars in pale blue burkas,
Infants cradled in their laps—
Winters in South Beach where the dead are dismembered in movie set crime labs.
All the pieces of the dead are posing for parts.

She eats gulab jamuns, the rosewater running down her arms.
She announces: Don't turn to salt. Don't face Mecca.
West Bank boys, undo your belts.
The Cairo street children with their horror B-movie doll heads under arm,
The Sunnis and the Shi'ites, their Almodovar electric drills in hand.

She opens up the doors to her library:
If one thing has meaning, then everything does.
We pick through a mountain of garbage, like loving.

Allergic

Assad sits at his desk, erasing his thoughts
With an assortment of sushi-shaped erasers.
The woman he longs for is half his age
At a desk so close he can smell her lotion

And the remains of a salad bar lunch scattered on her computer keyboard.
It is too early for headlines, sky azure.

She comes to him every day, avoiding work.

Alone in an oak-paneled elevator.
The numbers rise rapidly.
She smoothes the hem of her skirt,
Just an inch above the knee, running.

At home, his wife (an Armenian)
Refuses to be called by that title. She pats kibbeh,
Her hands scented with rose and ground lamb,
Scans the local paper for apartments.
The youngest child is not his, half-Palestinian.

As commuters run by, a vendor continues to hawk umbrellas
In the shape of the world.
Get 'em before it's too late.

The woman he longs for has straight black hair
That never, ever changes.

A DON'T WALK sign flashes, and the crowd gathers
At a safe distance.

Her skin is the color of a mirror.
She thinks he is very funny, without any pity.

The Armenian *knows* he has a sense of humor,
But it isn't enough. She wants a cat.

Suppertime, after Emil Nolde, Banksy, and the West Bank, 2003

Blue paint spills over the table
In baptism. Jesus is built like a wrestler,
Absent-mindedly squeezing
A water bottle in his thick sausage hands.
Everyone is going to get all wet.

A ladder painted up the height of the wall divides holiness.
The stars blister above it.
A man says, "You've made the wall beautiful, but we don't want it
To be beautiful."

My, Lord, don't you have big, fat, collagen lips,
Kim Basinger lips, all the better to swallow you with.

The evening wolf rides the crest of rocky hills, will not enter here.
There is a claque of bluebottle flies at a corpse; still the wolf won't come.

There is a man in a crimson robe with his arm
Around John. His hair is in a frenzy of curls.
He needs Burt's Bees' Avocado cream.
Whatever name you call him by
Is beautiful. He is a peace activist or a suicide bomber.

Fatima's eyes line the internet café.
The blow-fly necrologists go right up over the wall, easily.

Across the table, Jesus reaches out
To clasp the one he loved best. There is a triangle at this table,

And these three are not talking theology.

Come to Prayer, May 2007, Damascus to Beirut

Boys spill out of clubs, Marmar and Underground in Damascus at sunrise.
It was Muhammad who said, *Tear the bread with your teeth*.
The humidity cradles the verdant tangle of vines
Suspended in air, with lawful magic. The boys sleep till midday,
Filthy with the grime of night-before back rooms, sprawled
On old couches in the courtyard, wake and feast on dates and greasy fried kafta.
Sisters drop their barrette-clips of Syrian pounds from the windows by afternoon.
The boys shower and resume breathing.

       —A bomb went off in Verdun, in Beirut.
Friends call, checking in. One man who loves *love* presses on another at sunset
On the beach, the salty smell of the Mediterranean, the taste of figs
Between his legs, the cry of the minaret
Pulling him home to his apartment. He picks up the phone: *It's all right here.* Evening
Shadows lick up the walls, and the light licks
Back against shadow, as the police cordon off the scene on Dream TV.

Photograph of a Roma Orphan by the Curb

Broken glass and razor wire were the architecture that you cannot see.
She came out of the womb barefooted with metal crescents like moons
And scythes everywhere. She was roughed with uncles and lit cigarettes.
See, under the arms, a tattoo of burns she can't count.
She doesn't recognize
Terror: her dark hair flying up in panic,
Head hung so low to the ground, looking
Down at the dust that will cover our tongues.

Now she is two, named Coriander for a gift of prophecy.
She is crawling in a Berlin gutter.
She has the face of a dark moon and hair that lunges
Like the light of first evening stars.
She has no father or mother.
They must have despaired.
Every passerby looks down on her, and every dog looks down.
She lived at the edge of a passage with view of leg and shoe.
She looked bewildered. In heaven, there were no angels mounting a rescue mission.
This is a true story. There was an air raid.
She looks up at the voices from heaven calling out.
She lives in the gutter on the edge of a passage.
She will always be two. She will never get up.
She will beg forever from you.

Sam's Club

I have a silvery shopping cart.
It is full of tomato soup.

Box cutters clatter to the floor.
There is a long row reaching into the future.

I follow like Dorothy, red shoes clicking.

The cart weaves slightly, noiselessly,
To a ballroom waltz in strings.

I know I've had my fair share already.
But prices are slashed.

What Their Hands Had Sent Ahead

As if throwing a ball into air, you have lunged
Into the future of yourself. I cross the jetway;
Have I left you behind me? Owen, toddler
In your Mediterranean-blue shirt and toasted cheese with mustard—
What time is it in your home without me?
I'm coming back soon if the traffic of Damascus
Doesn't kill me.

This was before it got so bad.

Ahmet Hashim said, *Poetry is that which is lost in translation.*

The Italians would say, *traduttore, traditore:*
To translate we betray. It is unutterable,
The *spruch* of my son, sayings
Without corresponding statement.
He says and it is so.

I got lost.

The minaret is a signal and a warning, time to go back,
Time to go home. You can hold out against death
With a story, thousands.
There is no translation in the Umayyad mosque,
Only divine text, written over and over—

Listen, all it says is you.

Hit Biscuits

Impossible yellow of daffodils on the windowsill,
The wind in a tangle in the trees,

And it could be spring in any country. Except that the flowers are native.

His eyes look up at me while he sucks one nipple
And flicks the other with his finger.

He says as he sucks, *I won't stop, I won't stop*, and it's all I can do
Not to let him see me wince. My nipples feel mangled but are not.

Each time he crawls as he did the first time: up over my belly,
Wormlike.
But he grabs a breast with both hands now that he is older,

Latching on.
                    He'll eat me and leave me in his body for good.

It's the only way he can imagine being.

In Calcutta, a woman came to me carrying her baby:
A sack of bones, the one she'd chosen to die. It happens all the time.

His kohl-lined eyes rolled in their sockets. Saviors there are painted blue and never die.
Babies *do*. I gave her all the money in my pocket,
But to my memory she gave it back.

A little girl stood beside her,
Wearing only *Beauty and the Beast* underpants.

Her brown belly curved out at me in a question mark.

I gave her a red package of *Hit* chocolate-filled biscuits.
She smiled up at the mother who nodded, yes. And said, *Eat.*

Differences

I.

Curlicue of white lace on the cheap Czech curtains,
Each machine-stitched embellishment a pixilated, out-of-date thing.
As a pilgrim living in Damascus, she wanted her life to be romantic, full of the world:
A Didion Malibu, Miró, pygmy goats, Vietnamese coffee and croque-en-bouche.
She wanted everything, all of it.
Instead,
In the fluorescent glare she sees the unnatural green of a Spray 'N Wash bottle.
Everything is out of control, she said.
                                        The mural she painted apropos Picasso
Frightened the children.

Could she live in a hanging garden? Swim in a hamman? She made a vow:
Never to buy another ugly thing. This is difficult to do in the souk;
This is what she found there:

—Bravo laundry boxes hung from the awnings of a shop
—A boy wears a girls' embroidered shirt, sits on a pile of carpets
woven with the image of the Lion of Hezbollah
—A Hugo Chavez poster over rows of sticky apricots.

She'd have to use the Internet.

She would brush her teeth with reeds and avoid the plastic. She took out her telescope,

Searching for Pleiades, unable to discern where to look.
But against the smog curtain of haze and glare
She always found herself staring at the negative reflection of her own one eye.

2.

The bathroom floor is strewn with clothing
Like the scene of a mass murder, frantic
T-shirts with galloping horses, dizzying red and white
Gingham, fish with blue eyes gasping for breath
Or escape.

There is a trickle of garbage-choked water in the river Baruda, where Paul converted,
Was baptized.

It offers nothing.

At home in Iowa at the John Deere Play Place
The women in hijab and chadors ignored her.

Their children pulled at the hem of their skirts,
Somersaulted on the carpet.
Here in Damascus, the pilgrims to Husein stop her on the street, call out, extending arms
Out of their black abayas to embrace.

In Tehran, they say, *Fargh Phil Collins*—
                    such small differences between us.

Now she's surrounded by dirty apparel, drinking Croatian beer.
The day was too much for laundry. The boy wanted her to be a train.
The girl wanted her to hurry, hurry.

She sent them away with the father. *Khoob Biid? Is it Goooood?* asks the satellite television.

She fell into a greasy tub and dreamed—
                    buried up to her neck, death by stoning.

She was wrong about the souk. There was so much more:

The nargileh lighters, swinging their baskets, the nighttime glow of the embers.
The boy washing down the stone alcove in front of his father's shop.
The tiger skins, dried iguanas, and puffer fish.

Outside, the cricket song of summer.

          She had seen him earlier, in a rhyme or a tale, oud on his back.

It crawled into her mind with no idea
                    there could still be a song like that.

Song of Palaces

Shallow green water trips down the stone-terraced Miljacka,
Bats flap their frantic wings through the spotlights flooding
The burned-out hulk of the national library, and Sarajevo
Youth pour out of the mosques on their way to the Karabit café
For lemon sugar and orange sugar in their tea, or to Dveri
To drink juniper juice and listen to country songs on the veranda, "Redneck Woman."

Young mothers and fathers push strollers of crying babies or sleeping ones.
Grandmothers and old men, girls and boys stroll along the sidewalks of the Ferhadija,
Past the lights of Bennetton and Esprit, the call of the imam, the eternal flame waving its hands,
Over the Sarajevo roses, those shrapnel wounds in the sidewalk,
Filled in with red putty by art students. The pedestrians walk over the roses until midnight, back
And forth over the roses to Sloga to get drunk, to Café Brasil for white rum and sugar crêpes,
To Mash Club for a Halloween party.

Heading east toward Islamic Cairo, heading west downtown, beside the Nile,
The dry and dusty Khamsen blows the girls' scarves, rebel-winged.
They rocket from dust of dead men, rising in gowns as black as the coloring of God.
From the upper floor of the Ali Baba cafeteria, these wet, black angels
Conjure ways to fly, descending on the old men playing backgammon.
Down in the square, the couples run, linked arm in arm in the flare of lightning;
The hands of wind pull them to the east, farther than Islamic Cairo,
Toward the West, way beyond downtown. *He has proportioned all the skies*.

In Istanbul are spotlights of green light on mosque and minaret, and stars shoot out of the path.
The woman in her fringed hijab searches for her daughter who is shooting Raki.
O Kuba, covered in a grey blanket of snow, the color of intellectual films!
Another One Bites the Dust on the radio.

Tripoli! The cedars are spreading their chests to the luminous blue sky;
Slope and gorge split their skirts apart. The poet is buried in the old monastery town.
He could walk like Lazarus down to the candy capital of the world
And eat rosewater lokum and the resurrection.
Today boys are swimming naked in the cool waters under the waterfalls of the En-gedi,
Where the lovers sang in the Song of Songs.

I'll walk into the reeds where you are hiding, an insurgent.
I'll wash my hair until it turns to fire.
Let's turn over together in the reeds and the water.
We'll name the ducks their thousands of jewel names.
Not one martyr will be left standing after he's learned every name of every bird.

Ash-Shām

From the mountain, Jabal Qasiuon,
Above Damascus, God sees everything.

Not a hand over me, God says.
Sometimes he becomes Innana, *Mistress of the Me.*

His breasts swell at night with the lights of houses, asterisms
Scattered against the hill, a mirage of starry sky.

Below, on a rooftop in Yarmouk camp, a Palestinian boy
Washes his green and pink bicycle.

Down the broad traffic-choked avenue, the leaves of the trees
Recant all their summer promises.

The little rooms grow cold. Space heaters crackle to life.

A man in a shop smoothes velvet baby dresses
With his rough fingertips.

The laurel leaves, elderberry,
And arbors of jasmine are virescent memories, suspended.

God sees everything over ash-Sham, which is the real name
For Damascus, the ones who know will tell you—

And farther still, farther God looks with her necklace of eyes,
To where the call to prayer overlaps with other calls
From other directions,

Farther than the call to prayer can reach, to where in a cell, a man
Has written poetry on a Styrofoam cup with his fingertips,

About paradise:

The roar of music there, unceasing—

The light's execration—

The water, irremissible as it pours into breath—

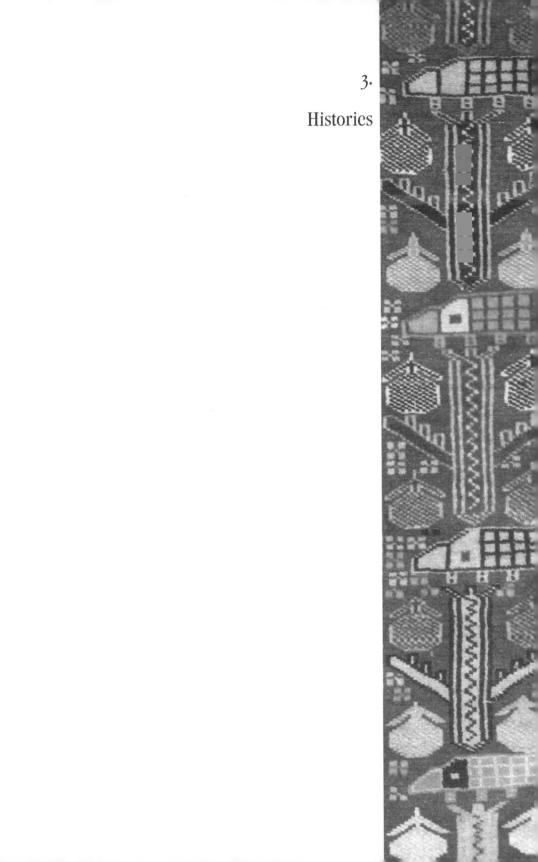

3.

Histories

Witchcraft in Twin Springs

I left the sliding glass door open in the basement all night,
And anyone could enter from the woods.

I always leave the car parked in the driveway facing out.

My mother has promised to *kill me if,* and she meant it.

She will wrap me in a plastic tarp and drop me down the spring pit,
The one where they buried the slaves, and it fell in. My stepfather
Covered it with plywood.

Virginia has so many graves in the suburbs. Some are Masters' good and bad,
Some are unmarked property.

My younger brother snuck out to meet with a coven
Down in the cul-de-sac. They carried bags of flour on their backs.

They drew circles and pentagrams, thirteen and casting spells with grown-ups.

It was the 8os. Everyone was doing it.

Down in the kitchen, night-light lit, I opened the drawer of knives.

The cats mewing at the basement door, let us out, out.

Anatomy

I went to see the bodies at the Field Museum.
One leapt through space to catch a ball.
He was a still hover, red giant flame, unflickering.
One, a man of nerves and sinew, rode a flayed horse off the Mongolian steppes
And reared above me, an Apollyon in a pit.

Is it possible to fill in the blanks after all that touch?
The answer is, *of course*. The doctor of dentistry I met at a dinner party
Said so. Adam said that it is easy to eat a sandwich in one hand and articulate
With another. He would take me and show me. You must summon
And then chase the dead away.
I wanted to, so I did it.

I might have gone further, made a gesture, given up all of literature, the tap and tack-toe
Of machines that write, to baby massage a dead baby on a board, to touch it
Barehanded. I would find answers to questions without any need of punctuation.
But would I understand anything at all, bookless? Since we have insisted
On replacing the anatomy lesson with the book. We won't cut without it open.

We have cable television, and I saw a documentary about Jeffrey Dahmer.
He was hit in the head when he was very young! Did anyone do an autopsy?
I feel so bad, but worried because I sometimes want to collect dead animals myself,
For various art projects and protestations.
I read the book *The Sociopath Next Door,* and it did not apply to me.

What else can I do: heap hot coals, draw in the sand, light some resin, make a book.
I'll do
Everything, everything

Just to touch you.

Get Ready

In three years, Jesus will be here.
Our neighbors are getting ready.
Mrs. Halteman and her five girls
All wear identical calicos.
The two boys kneel on one knee
Like little men in hats.
They are very happy and say,
Keep looking up!
                          I don't. I gave
The venison they gave me to a friend
Who doesn't believe in God but had
A Pentecostal upbringing. I'm not
One for wild meat.

My mother claims she can just *tell*
When someone's a believer. I think
It's their accent.

My high school social studies teacher
Had a picture of Jesus laughing,
His smile overextended
Like a sideways fun house mirror.
                          My husband
Does not believe in Jesus.
I'm afraid he'll wake in the night a demon,
His face masked with hilarity and alarm,
Like Jack Nicholson in *The Shining*.
They say demons are allowed to do that
With unbelievers.

Valerie's Threat

I no longer speak to my stepfather,
But he passed this letter along.
She's thinking up ways to kill me.
She's driving up Interstate 95
With a butcher knife in her black
Honda Accord. She's listening to
Pet Shop Boys.
                  Meanwhile,
I'm at Stringtown grocery
Buying sorghum and piccalilli. Black
Amish buggies in a row. Field stubble
Pokes through the snow.

My stepfather accuses me of resembling
My mother. In the mirror,
There is no reflection.

Now, at home I'm making pfefferneusse.
Valerie is waiting in the cellar.
When my husband returns,
The kitchen will be slick with blood.
I'll be mostly chopped up.

Lost

You love me with Jesus. *I'm* no Jew.
You love me in Laguna Beach,
California daddy. Morning glories
Tangle all along your driveway.
Hummingbirds buzz with panic.
My sandy blonde hair in salted tangles,
You love me with the glass coffee table
Full of sand and seashells. It never rains
In our childhood. We don't read books.
There's a hammock and 70s hit record,
Long polyester pointed collars,
Everything spinning in the mind's
Category of forgotten. Love me
In Bethlehem, Pennsylvania, in our people's
Horse-drawn buggy, your long dark curls
Like slivers of Hershey's chocolate. Daddy,
Where'd you get that dimple in your chin?
I wish you were Jewish.
Love me at Jolly Rogers in a pirate hat.
Love me at La Brea tar pits
Where the dinosaur dead go down, stuck
With a hundred thousand years yet
To catch up on. He is dead and gone.

Milk

When I was a girl, I felt ashamed.
It was the commercials for milk.
I didn't drink milk.
There was one about a swimming pool
Full of milk, which was the worst
Because I couldn't swim either.

My brother dragged me across the Rappahannock.
It sucked me under. It thrust me up. It sucked me under.
He held to the back of my neck, knuckles clenched.
He saved me.

The Holy Spirit convicts us. It moves through
The congregation with the sound of Brother Bob's voice:
Every head bowed. Every eye closed. No one looking around.

I know it's me. I'm the one who hiked up my skirt,
Pretending to sleep. I'm the one who shoplifted
The vintage flapper and ran peeing down Caroline Street.

My brother drinks a lot of milk.
He has a car stereo for dating.
My father asked, What did you think of the sermon?
Grace, women are graceful. Submit.
I thought it was disgusting, said the half-girl, furious.
I think *you're disgusting*, said her dad, infuriated.

A Sony Trinitron

Encased in matte black plastic. It looks new, right out of the box.

The television beeps softly and crackles to itself.

A small rainbow splays across the kitchen wall.

We wake up hours before the alarms.

Dad tumbled down the brand-new deck attached to our house in suburban Philadelphia.

Was Mom a morning person? Smoking a Kool in her nightgown, watching the *Today Show*.

I sat on a stool at the kitchen counter, a steaming bowl of farina before me.

I slap the clock, slip out of my robe. The coffee pot is clogged.

Dark amber pools.

Wondering if it's safe to unplug the machine.

Testimonies

I am just a girl from Virginia. I don't know much.
I learned runes and hieroglyphs and wanted
To be a philologist, I told the first girl
I ever slept with. In church, I wrote every word
I could remember from *Alpha* to *Omega*.
We were forbidden from going to prom together.
The English teacher crossed our names off the list.

My name was erased from its original birth certificate.
In its place was typed another. It's called *adoption*.
My Daddy I was born to became a name, *Woody*.
He was thrown out of the pulpit: *hypocrites,*
Brood of vipers! His sermons were not well received.

We sang this hymn at twelve: "Power in the Blood,"
Giggling hysterically. My sins went down with Christ
Under red, blue, and white spotlights: the Blood,
The Death, the Resurrection. The hair dryers screamed
Like seraphim and cherubim in the girls' bathroom.
Could you see my nipples through my wet, white gown?
Could you see any blood on me? Daddy had transfigured
From me while I was still in patent shoes with a plastic
Orange bowl on my head for a hat. Words are inconsolable.
My memory smells of Noxzema. When we left him behind,
He became a name, a-men, a name, say it again.

Undecidable

Jesus, when I dream of You,
You wear a Klein-blue dress, small-waisted and flared.
Your feet are perfect with a French manicure, no wounds.
Your long chestnut-brown hair is pulled up like a Guess
Supermodel on a motorcycle in the back alleys of Rome.

It's not that you are a woman, God forbid.

For instance, when you ascend the stairs up and out of the subway into the heavenly light
Of Dupont Circle, everyone stares as you rise again, so beautifully, irretrievably, You.

When my stepdad is done from here, would you take him home with you?
I hope you and he will find a nice place to lay your heads.
Smooth out his pregnant beer-belly. Make it firm.
His puma-colored hair make radiant like obsidian.
Feed him Kalamata olives.
Scrape his body with olive oil, personally.

Trade his graying Fruit of the Looms for H&M boxer briefs,
The color of angel wings, like his newly whitened teeth.
Bend down on your knees. Unscrew the lid of Revlon's Oxblood Red,
And paint all ten of his toes.

The Pelican

My father, whom I did not know at the time,
Was at Yelapa Bay, Mexico.
He had been missing since I was seven. One day,
He came around a bend and found a wounded pelican,
Caught on a fishing line, tangled and hooked.
Every time the bird thrust its head back,
The pouch tore,
The hook ripped a little bit more, an episiotomy
That birthed only fear.
It wasn't the first time. Once, he'd led a deer
Just like the father in Arabian nights with the gazelle,
Who bought a third of a life for a stranger.
My father sat near through her labor
Until she gave birth.

The pelican would die. About this time I would have
Wondered where he was, if near.
My father, whom I was beginning to forget,
Crept low to the ground in a gesture of humility the bird recognized,
Beyond all believability, and calmed.
My father, who left when I was very young, cradled the pelican in his arms.
My father was a ticket agent for Braniff airlines
And always carried his sewing kit in his pocket.
He was prepared for anything but fatherhood.
But at the bend in the bay he mended the hurt bird.

Homesick

When the dove was an egg,
It had no bone. We are not at all certain.

I will one day fly out of the second story
Of the house that is painted Persian Gulf blue,

Or toothpaste colored, into a midwestern sky
The same hue.

I'll fly like Ianna moving swiftly across the sky,
Swinging her frilled, night skirts.

I want to go back. Where I left my one sequined shoe in the crawfish hole,
Gone forever. I'll pull it out like a tooth and mate it.

I will eat rhododendrons.
I will fall over Blue Ridge Mountain rock.
Now I'm dreaming.

Or am I as awake as a childhood question?

There were pigeons in the rafters where I slept.
I was a runaway with all the boys. I miss their cooing.

Looking up over the farmers' fields is Fatima's eye reflected back, a blue flag
Of warning. The blackbirds are distracted.

In the woods of my lost shoe, nothing can find you. You're permanently lost.

The Test

I.

I lost my virginity on a faux-leather couch in Brother Bob's office.
It smeared, the color of bearberry.

I was walking up the sidewalk, awash
In the glow of lampposts. A man snatched me like a plastic

Lawn ornament, a gnome or rabbit. He stuffed me in the trunk.

Once, my brother came face to face with a cottonmouth in the creek.

He got away simply by walking backwards. It didn't work for me.

2.

In Cairo, the tampons are kept behind the counter. The children chase
After, screaming, *Broken! Broken!*

There is a Marc Chagall hanging somewhere in Cairo: A rabbi pinching snuff.

Show me the text. I showed you mine, in the palm of my hand.
Show me the text, rabbi. I'm dying to understand.

The Headship Veiling

I wore a head covering made of white.
But it is worn out, the color of semen.

The corn whispers, *Lost*.
Children cannot find their way out of there.

When I became a woman,
It was so difficult to learn French.
I ride a motor scooter in a striped shirt,
Breathless with my bad guy, killer, thief.

I went to Algiers and wore the veil.
I cut off my hair with a saw.
I have a boy. I never hurt him.

Some mornings I make him pancakes
In the shape of the letter *A*.

Warnings

The Haida, Tlingit used the moss as diapers.
Skunk cabbage unfolds provocatively, the color of bad urine.
Bears eat it.
Rhododendrons, fiddlehead ferns,

                    Watch out, danger, extended forest floor.

Host trees and nurse logs,
The empty O where life ate out other life and left.

Bench: *In loving memory of lovely, gentle Sarah*
Who died here in her Dad's arms after a fall.

Douglas firs erupt into the canopy, marching giants;
The blind man said, *I see people like trees walking*
Or trees like people walking.

The salmon die, reddening flesh, mouldering eyes.
I carry my baby on my back, like the first ones,
Constantly walking out of frame.

                To die into mud and decay, disappear,

Drawn up into cypress,

Seymour spruce, grouse, salmon, it's okay, it's okay, there's no one then to blame.

The Wedding

I.

I'm the guest at a Sabean Mandaen wedding.

We gather at the public swimming pool,
The large rectangle dry and abandoned behind us.

The bride, wrapped in white mantles,
Goes down under the cold water in the kiddie pool, baptized.

On this frigid Damascus winter's day,
The stone patio glows with fragility.

On the courtyard wall is an old German clock carved of Black Forest wood.

In the waterless pool, mermaids splash against the walls,
Donald Duck casts a fishing rod. Stenciled seagulls swoop.

The sunlight, hot on my back,
Interrupts the forty-degree air,

Illuminates the tiles and the smooth linen
Of the priest's robes waist deep in the water.

The water spreads out before her, effulgent.

The bride flexes her hand against the cold,
Palm outstretched like the charm of Fatima, warning.

The family and friends crowd in,
Cell phones outstretched, lucent.

The crowd presses toward the bride.
The water bursts with sunlight.
My face hurts from squinting.

The priest tells the creation story:
From water to radiance to light, overflowing.

Sun boats and moon ships sail,
Like Nuh, who impossibly built his ark
And sailed the tempest. And John the Baptist,
Who was, from the beginning, the living water.

2.

There is no sea near this place, no boats.

The bride and groom are ready.

The priest slips the red rings and the green rings over their fingers,
Recalling the lights on the port and starboard of a ship.

As the bride exits, a little girl, prepubescent, walks backward before her,
Holding a mirror:
> *Look at yourself.*

Pomegranate twigs are scattered at her feet.

At my wedding, we had bowls of sycamore seeds,
Spray-painted golden.

She holds a myrtle wreath between her hands.

My wedding dress cost fifty dollars. I bought it off the mannequin.

I did a little leap when I said, *I do*. The guests laughed.

We had a potluck and a hymn sing in the fellowship hall.

In the baptismal pool is the chiaroscuro of evanescent light
And the dark upturned bellies of dead leaves.

3.

They turn to me, the guest, so excited that I grew up Baptist.
They want me to sing a hymn.

Before my marriage, I cut my favorite hymns
From the *Gospel Hymnal of Praise and Worship*
And mailed them to my husband-to-be.

I wanted him to remember the songs of my childhood and adolescence.

Rana, an Iraqi insurgent in green eyeliner, urges me to sing.
I might give offense if I refuse; but now, in the courtyard of the Sabean,
I cannot remember even one song.

Reading Rainbow

He's going down in a little hole.
I hope that now will last a while longer.
The smell of pine needles is like the taste of blood.
Owen says, *There's something terrible on the television*.
A cadaver on a board draining its fluids.
Lavar Burton comforts us aboard a camel.
It is educational.
The snow owl is calling or warning.
Let's go for a walk now,
While it is still light out.

Notes

Strangers (Ghurab): Italics are lines of graffiti found on some old Damascene houses and can be found in *Myths, Historical Archetypes and Symbolic Figures in Arabic Literature* (Franz Steiner, 1999). The line "My homeland is not a traveling bag" is from *Unfortunately, It Was Paradise*, Darwish (University of California Press, 2003), 69.

Chador: Italics are from fragments of Kurdish poetry by Jaziri.

Bit: Italics are from the poem "Martyr" by Mirawdeli.

Differences: Italics are from a popular TV show in Tehran, *Nights of Barareh*.

Ash-Shām: *"Not a hand over me"* from *A Time Between Ashes and Roses,* Adonis, (Syracuse University Press, 2004), 105.

Internally Displaced: Italics refers to the title of Wolfgang Tillman's photography show.

About the Author

Heather Derr-Smith was born in Dallas, Texas in 1971. She spent most of her childhood in Fredericksburg, Virginia. She earned her BA in art history from the University of Virginia and went on to earn her MFA in poetry writing from the Iowa Writers' Workshop. Her poems have appeared in *Fence, Margie, New York Quarterly*, and *TriQuarterly*. Her first book of poems, *Each End of the World* (2005), was about the war in Bosnia in the 1990s.

About the Book

The Bride Minaret was designed and typeset by Amy Freels. The typeface, ITC Garamond Book Condensed, is based on the types of Claude Garamond and was designed by Tony Stan for the International Typeface Corporation. It was released in 1976–1977.

The Bride Minaret was printed on 60-pound Natural Offset and bound by McNaughton & Gunn of Saline, Michigan.